This Log Belongs to:

A

Website
User Name
Password
Email Used
Notes

Website
User Name
Password
Email Used
Notes

Website
User Name
Password
Email Used
Notes

A

Website
User Name
Password
Email Used
Notes

Website
User Name
Password
Email Used
Notes

Website
User Name
Password
Email Used
Notes

A

Website
User Name
Password
Email Used
Notes

Website
User Name
Password
Email Used
Notes

Website
User Name
Password
Email Used
Notes

A

Website
User Name
Password
Email Used
Notes

Website
User Name
Password
Email Used
Notes

Website
User Name
Password
Email Used
Notes

B

Website
User Name
Password
Email Used
Notes

Website
User Name
Password
Email Used
Notes

Website
User Name
Password
Email Used
Notes

B

Website
User Name
Password
Email Used
Notes

Website
User Name
Password
Email Used
Notes

Website
User Name
Password
Email Used
Notes

B

Website
User Name
Password
Email Used
Notes

Website
User Name
Password
Email Used
Notes

Website
User Name
Password
Email Used
Notes

B

Website

User Name

Password

Email Used

Notes

Website

User Name

Password

Email Used

Notes

Website

User Name

Password

Email Used

Notes

C

Website
User Name
Password
Email Used
Notes

Website
User Name
Password
Email Used
Notes

Website
User Name
Password
Email Used
Notes

C

Website
User Name
Password
Email Used
Notes

Website
User Name
Password
Email Used
Notes

Website
User Name
Password
Email Used
Notes

C
Website
User Name
Password
Email Used
Notes
Website
User Name
Password
Email Used
Notes
Website
User Name
Password
Email Used
Notes

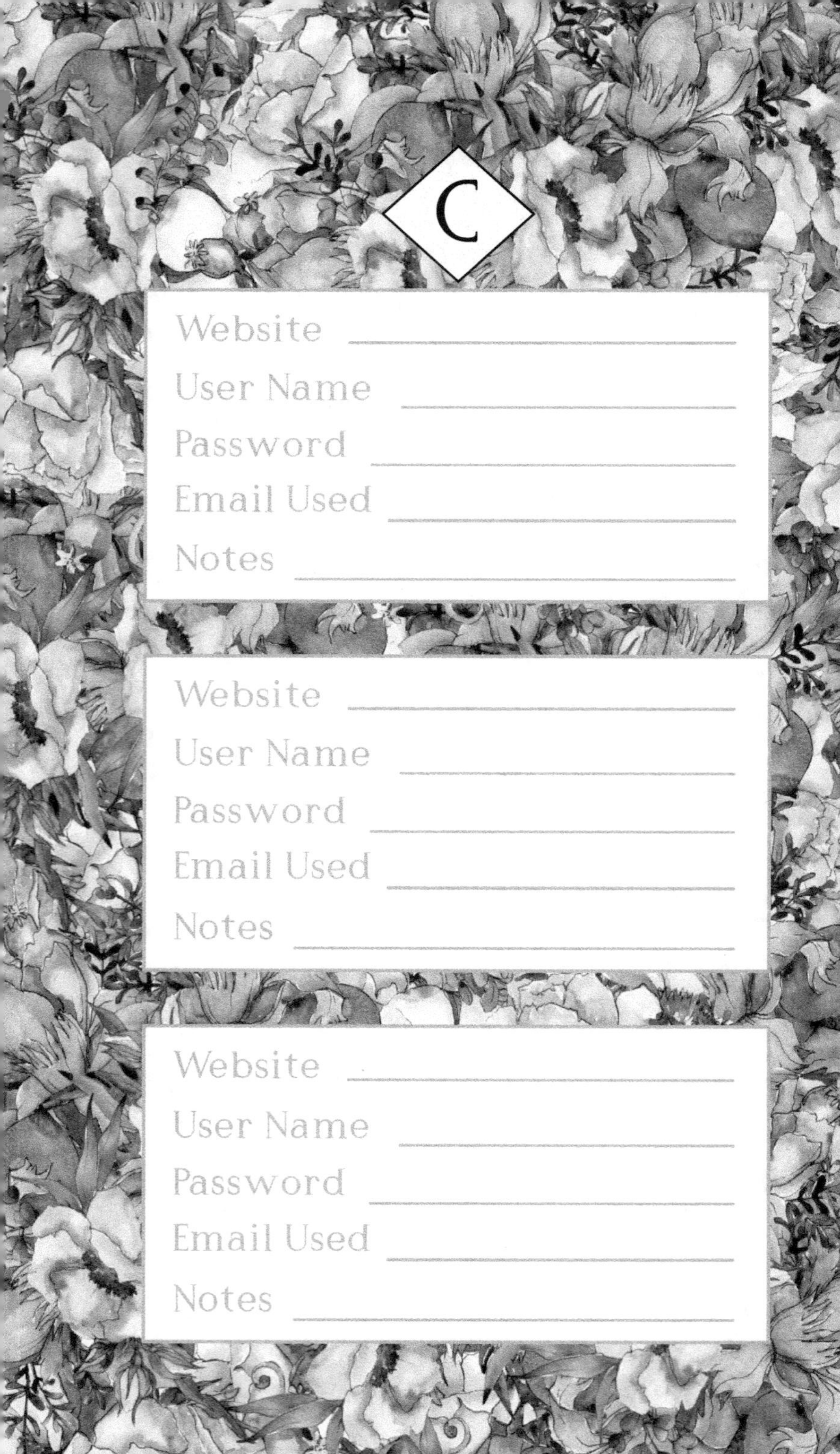

C

Website
User Name
Password
Email Used
Notes

Website
User Name
Password
Email Used
Notes

Website
User Name
Password
Email Used
Notes

D

Website

User Name

Password

Email Used

Notes

Website

User Name

Password

Email Used

Notes

Website

User Name

Password

Email Used

Notes

D

Website
User Name
Password
Email Used
Notes

Website
User Name
Password
Email Used
Notes

Website
User Name
Password
Email Used
Notes

D

Website
User Name
Password
Email Used
Notes

Website
User Name
Password
Email Used
Notes

Website
User Name
Password
Email Used
Notes

D

Website
User Name
Password
Email Used
Notes

Website
User Name
Password
Email Used
Notes

Website
User Name
Password
Email Used
Notes

E

Website

User Name

Password

Email Used

Notes

Website

User Name

Password

Email Used

Notes

Website

User Name

Password

Email Used

Notes

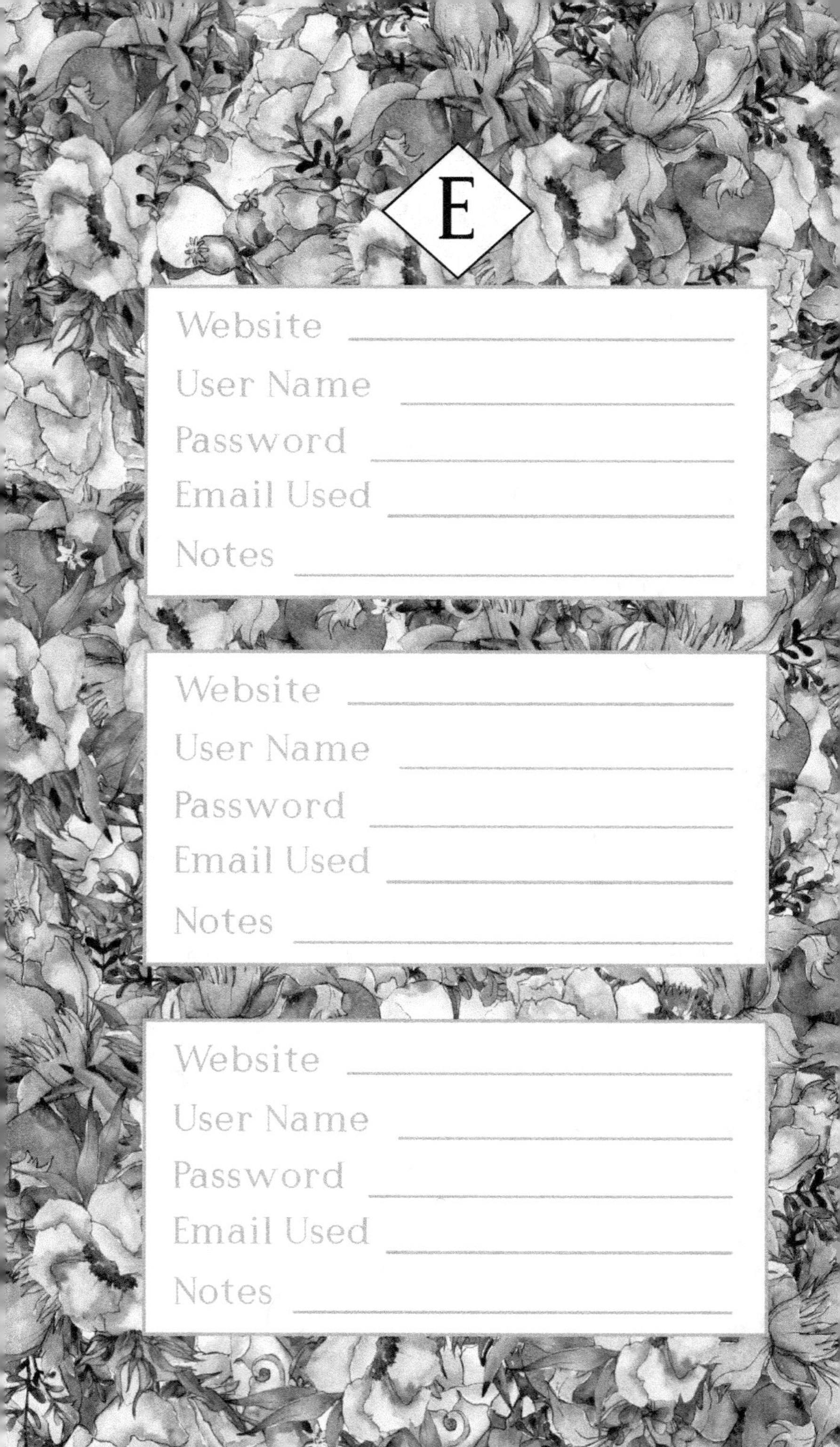
E

Website
User Name
Password
Email Used
Notes

Website
User Name
Password
Email Used
Notes

Website
User Name
Password
Email Used
Notes

E

Website

User Name

Password

Email Used

Notes

Website

User Name

Password

Email Used

Notes

Website

User Name

Password

Email Used

Notes

# E

Website

User Name

Password

Email Used

Notes

Website

User Name

Password

Email Used

Notes

Website

User Name

Password

Email Used

Notes

F

Website

User Name

Password

Email Used

Notes

Website

User Name

Password

Email Used

Notes

Website

User Name

Password

Email Used

Notes

F

Website
User Name
Password
Email Used
Notes

Website
User Name
Password
Email Used
Notes

Website
User Name
Password
Email Used
Notes

F

Website ______________________________
User Name ______________________________
Password ______________________________
Email Used ______________________________
Notes ______________________________

Website ______________________________
User Name ______________________________
Password ______________________________
Email Used ______________________________
Notes ______________________________

Website ______________________________
User Name ______________________________
Password ______________________________
Email Used ______________________________
Notes ______________________________

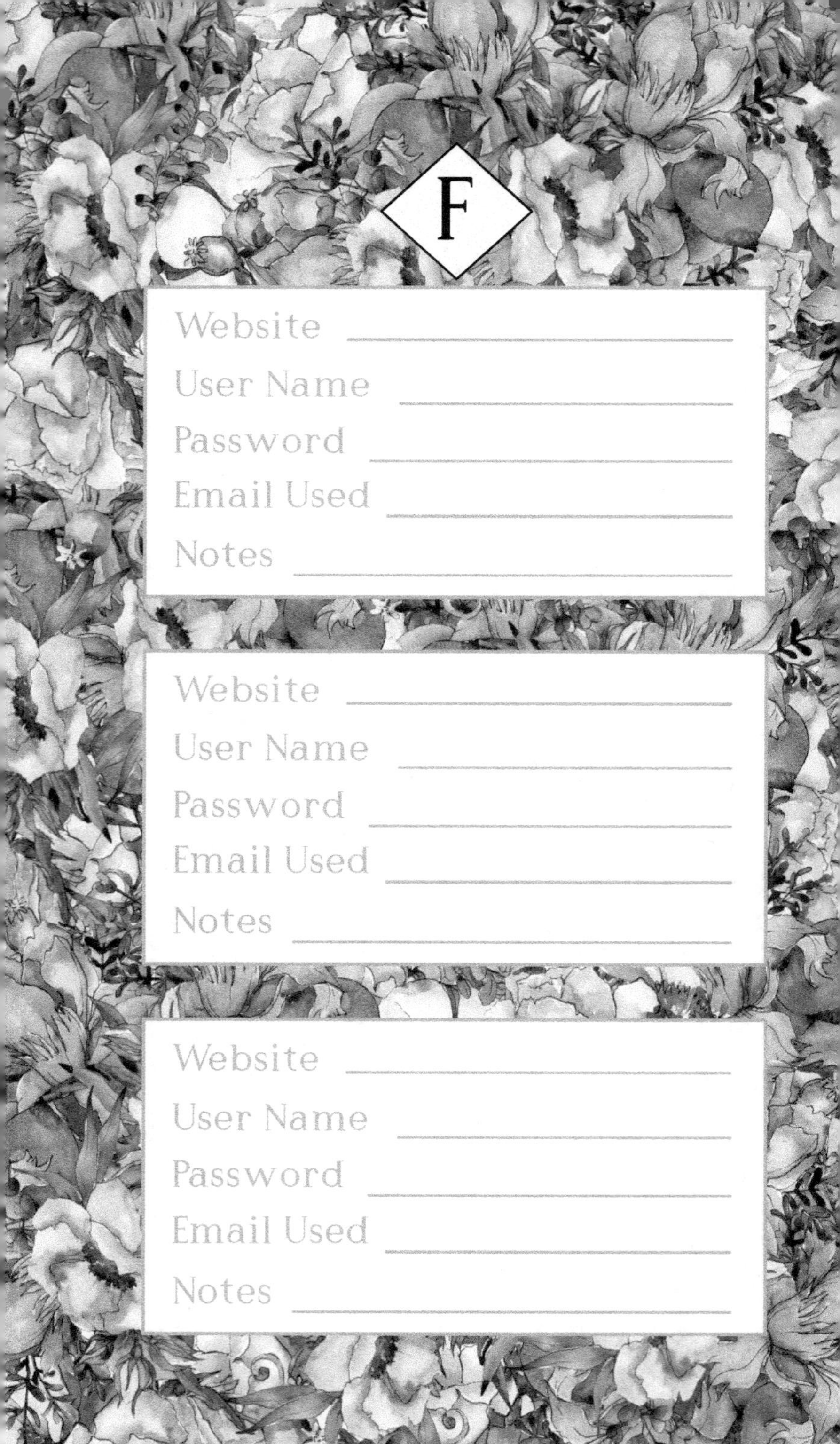

F

Website

User Name

Password

Email Used

Notes

Website

User Name

Password

Email Used

Notes

Website

User Name

Password

Email Used

Notes

G

Website
User Name
Password
Email Used
Notes

Website
User Name
Password
Email Used
Notes

Website
User Name
Password
Email Used
Notes

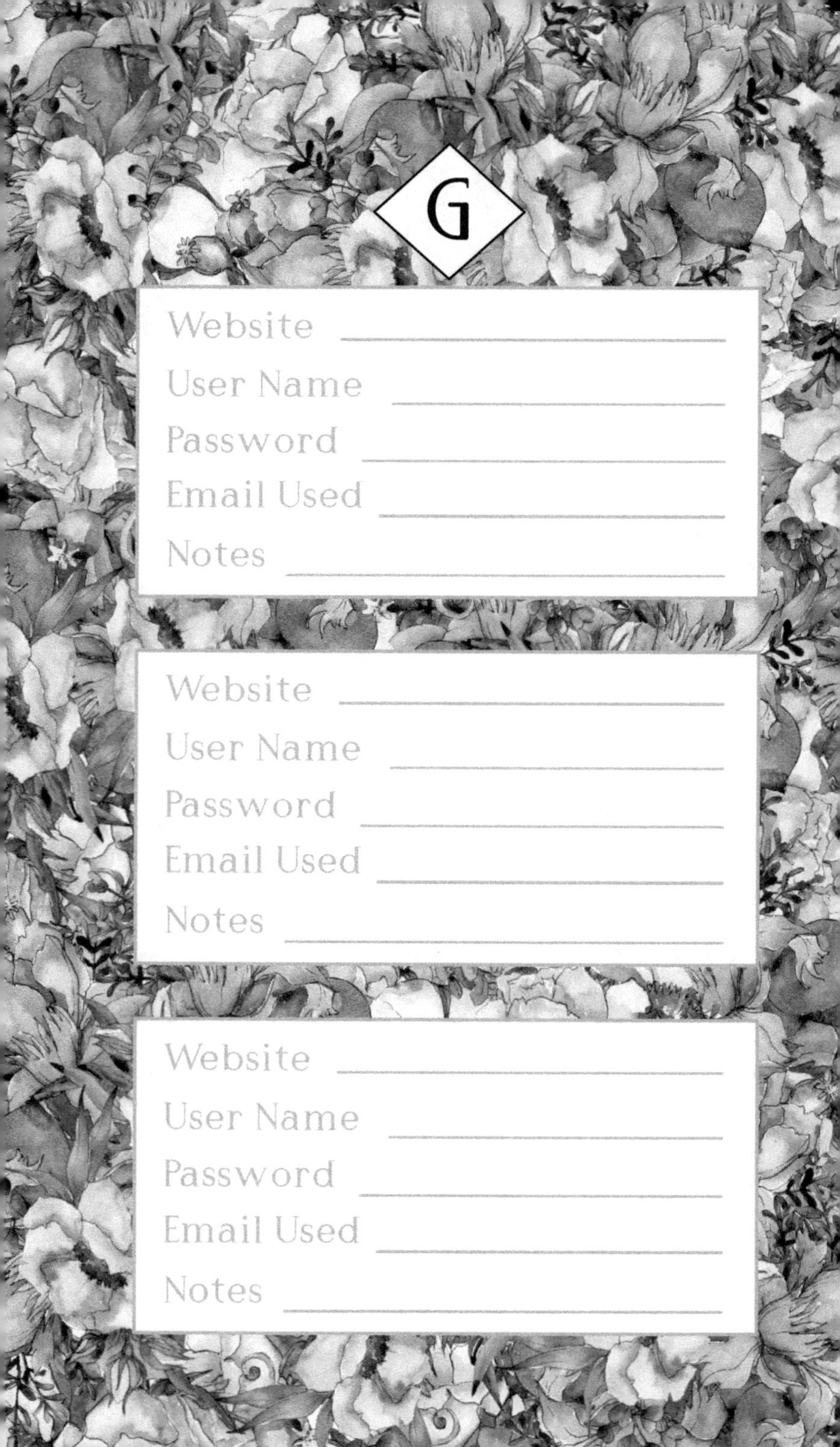
G

Website
User Name
Password
Email Used
Notes

Website
User Name
Password
Email Used
Notes

Website
User Name
Password
Email Used
Notes

G

Website
User Name
Password
Email Used
Notes

Website
User Name
Password
Email Used
Notes

Website
User Name
Password
Email Used
Notes

G

Website
User Name
Password
Email Used
Notes

Website
User Name
Password
Email Used
Notes

Website
User Name
Password
Email Used
Notes

H

Website
User Name
Password
Email Used
Notes

Website
User Name
Password
Email Used
Notes

Website
User Name
Password
Email Used
Notes

H

Website
User Name
Password
Email Used
Notes

Website
User Name
Password
Email Used
Notes

Website
User Name
Password
Email Used
Notes

H

Website
User Name
Password
Email Used
Notes

Website
User Name
Password
Email Used
Notes

Website
User Name
Password
Email Used
Notes

H

Website
User Name
Password
Email Used
Notes

Website
User Name
Password
Email Used
Notes

Website
User Name
Password
Email Used
Notes

I

Website

User Name

Password

Email Used

Notes

Website

User Name

Password

Email Used

Notes

Website

User Name

Password

Email Used

Notes

I

Website
User Name
Password
Email Used
Notes

Website
User Name
Password
Email Used
Notes

Website
User Name
Password
Email Used
Notes

I

Website _______________________

User Name _______________________

Password _______________________

Email Used _______________________

Notes _______________________

Website _______________________

User Name _______________________

Password _______________________

Email Used _______________________

Notes _______________________

Website _______________________

User Name _______________________

Password _______________________

Email Used _______________________

Notes _______________________

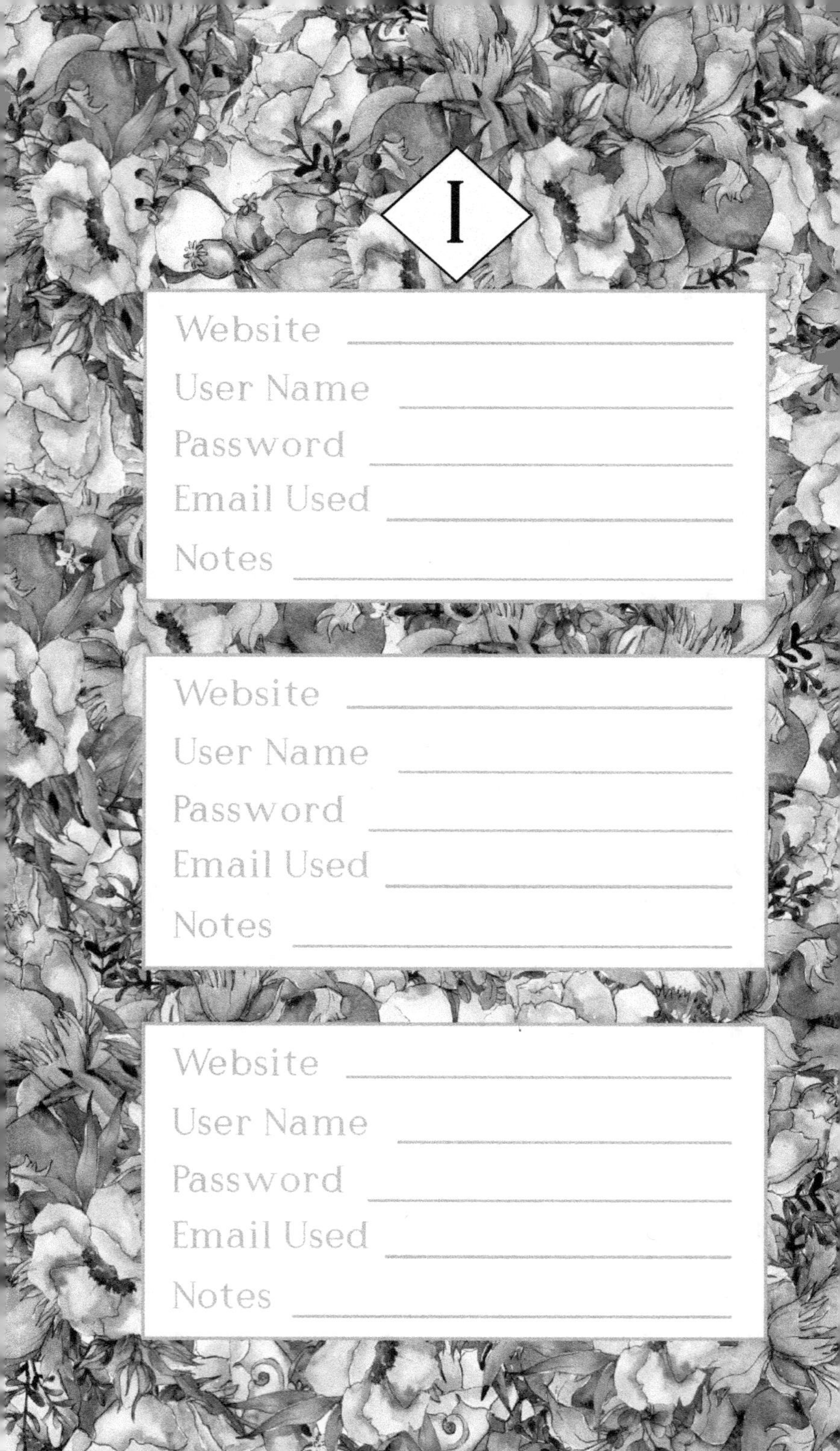

I

Website

User Name

Password

Email Used

Notes

Website

User Name

Password

Email Used

Notes

Website

User Name

Password

Email Used

Notes

J

Website
User Name
Password
Email Used
Notes

Website
User Name
Password
Email Used
Notes

Website
User Name
Password
Email Used
Notes

J

Website
User Name
Password
Email Used
Notes

Website
User Name
Password
Email Used
Notes

Website
User Name
Password
Email Used
Notes

J

Website
User Name
Password
Email Used
Notes

Website
User Name
Password
Email Used
Notes

Website
User Name
Password
Email Used
Notes

J

Website

User Name

Password

Email Used

Notes

Website

User Name

Password

Email Used

Notes

Website

User Name

Password

Email Used

Notes

K

Website

User Name

Password

Email Used

Notes

Website

User Name

Password

Email Used

Notes

Website

User Name

Password

Email Used

Notes

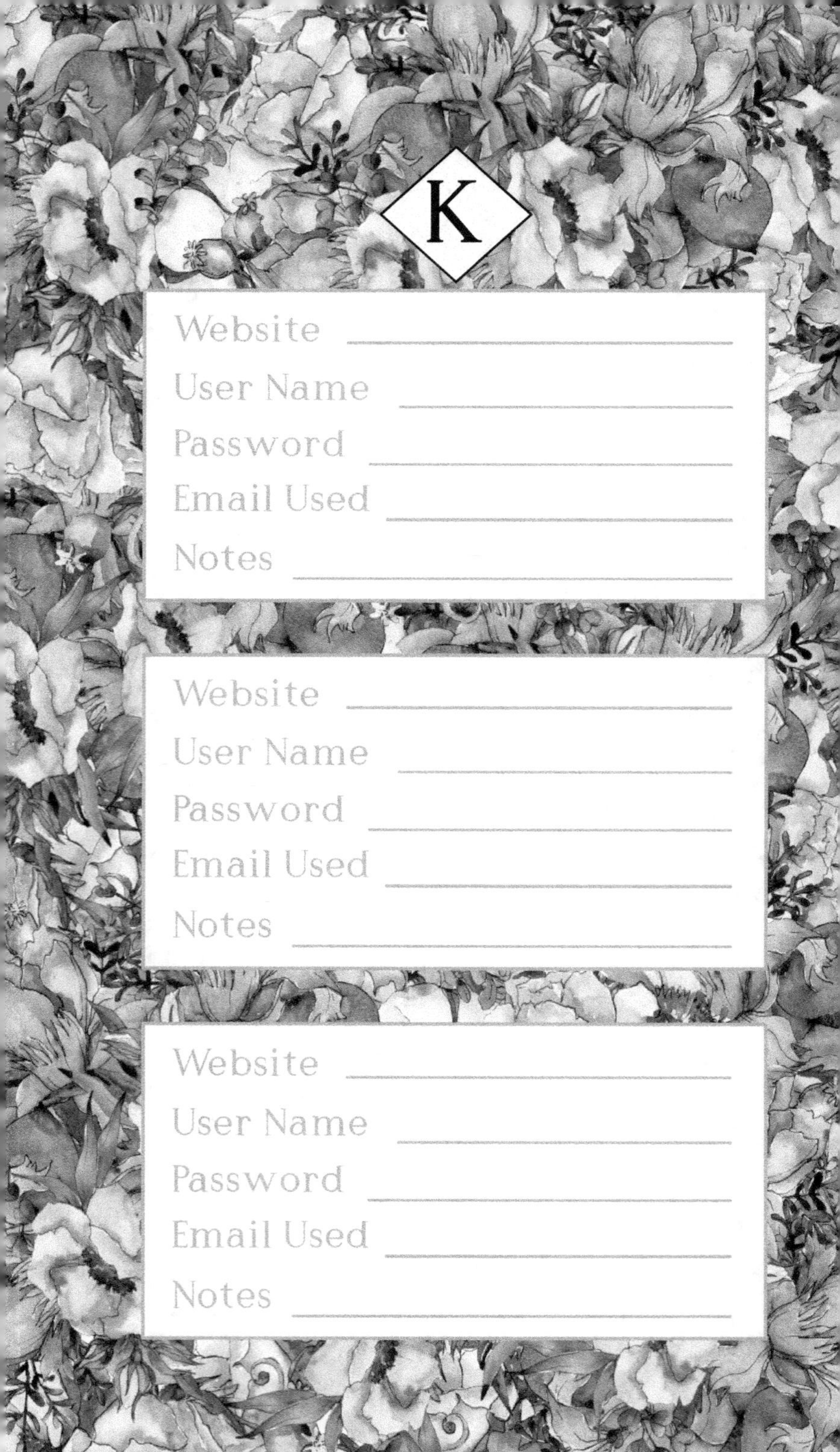

K

Website ___________________________
User Name ___________________________
Password ___________________________
Email Used ___________________________
Notes ___________________________

Website ___________________________
User Name ___________________________
Password ___________________________
Email Used ___________________________
Notes ___________________________

Website ___________________________
User Name ___________________________
Password ___________________________
Email Used ___________________________
Notes ___________________________

K

Website
User Name
Password
Email Used
Notes

Website
User Name
Password
Email Used
Notes

Website
User Name
Password
Email Used
Notes

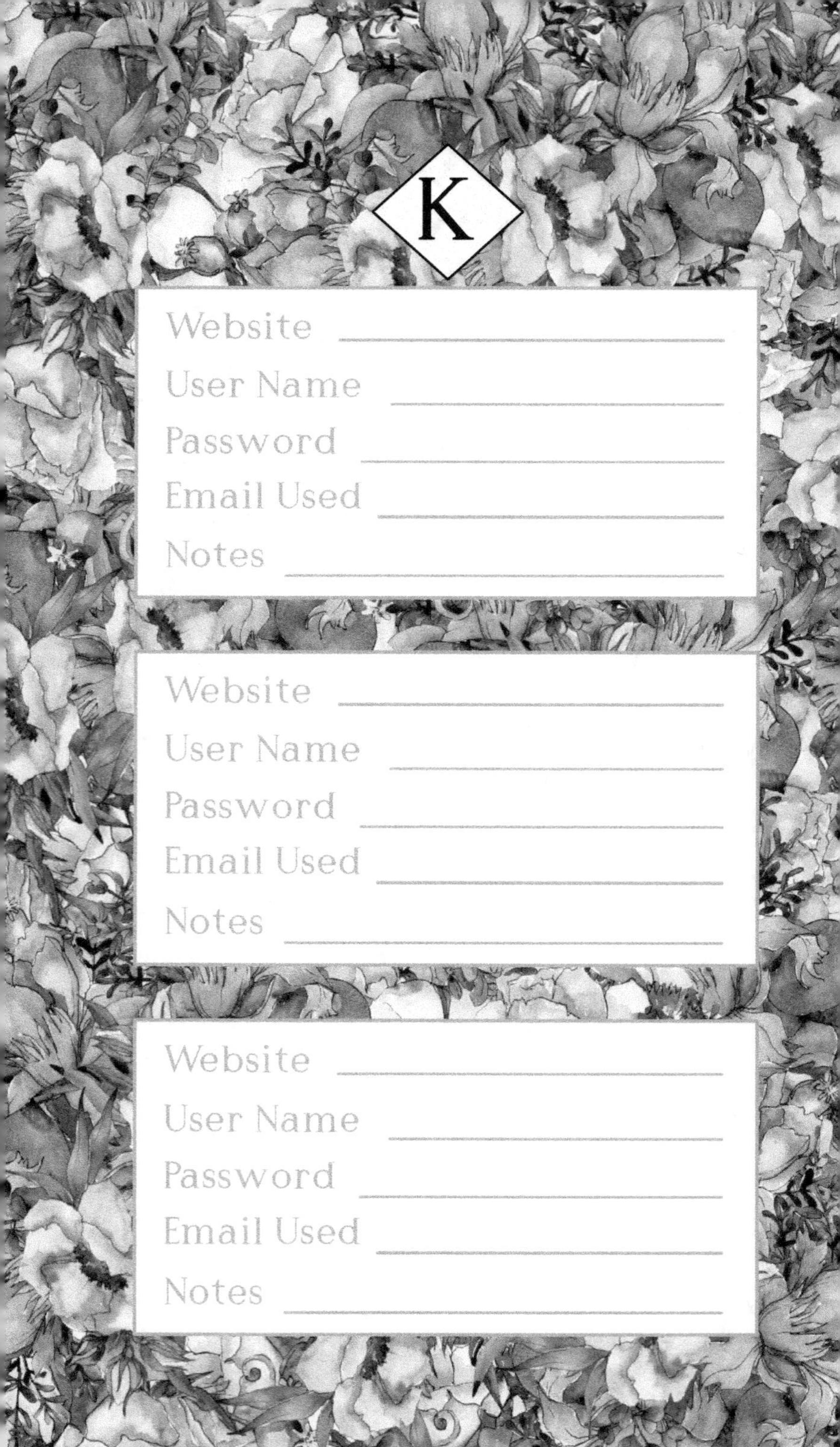

K

Website

User Name

Password

Email Used

Notes

Website

User Name

Password

Email Used

Notes

Website

User Name

Password

Email Used

Notes

L

Website ___________________________

User Name ___________________________

Password ___________________________

Email Used ___________________________

Notes ___________________________

Website ___________________________

User Name ___________________________

Password ___________________________

Email Used ___________________________

Notes ___________________________

Website ___________________________

User Name ___________________________

Password ___________________________

Email Used ___________________________

Notes ___________________________

L

Website

User Name

Password

Email Used

Notes

Website

User Name

Password

Email Used

Notes

Website

User Name

Password

Email Used

Notes

L

Website
User Name
Password
Email Used
Notes

Website
User Name
Password
Email Used
Notes

Website
User Name
Password
Email Used
Notes

L

Website

User Name

Password

Email Used

Notes

Website

User Name

Password

Email Used

Notes

Website

User Name

Password

Email Used

Notes

M

Website
User Name
Password
Email Used
Notes

Website
User Name
Password
Email Used
Notes

Website
User Name
Password
Email Used
Notes

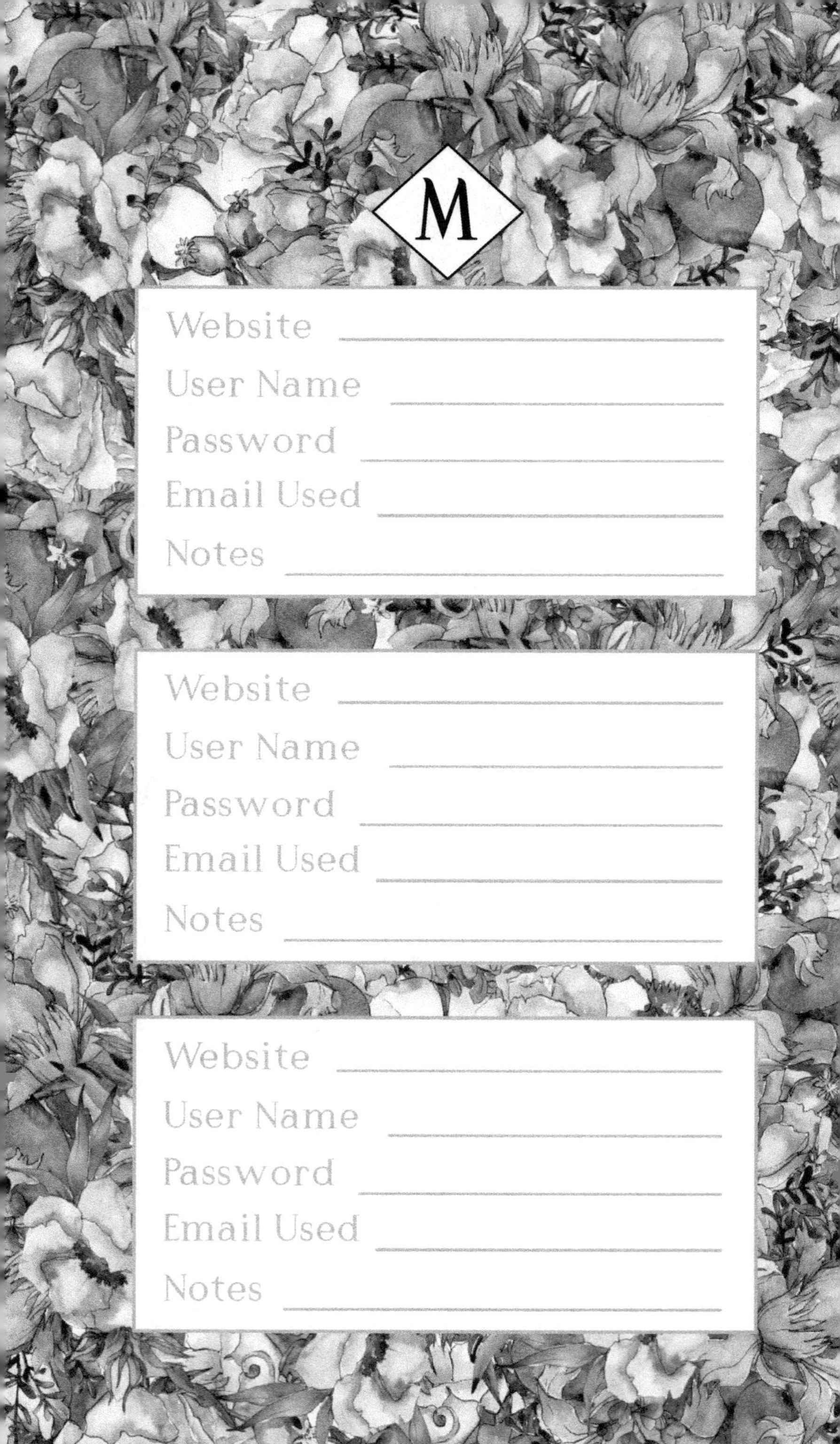
M

Website
User Name
Password
Email Used
Notes

Website
User Name
Password
Email Used
Notes

Website
User Name
Password
Email Used
Notes

M

Website
User Name
Password
Email Used
Notes

Website
User Name
Password
Email Used
Notes

Website
User Name
Password
Email Used
Notes

M

Website
User Name
Password
Email Used
Notes

Website
User Name
Password
Email Used
Notes

Website
User Name
Password
Email Used
Notes

N

Website

User Name

Password

Email Used

Notes

Website

User Name

Password

Email Used

Notes

Website

User Name

Password

Email Used

Notes

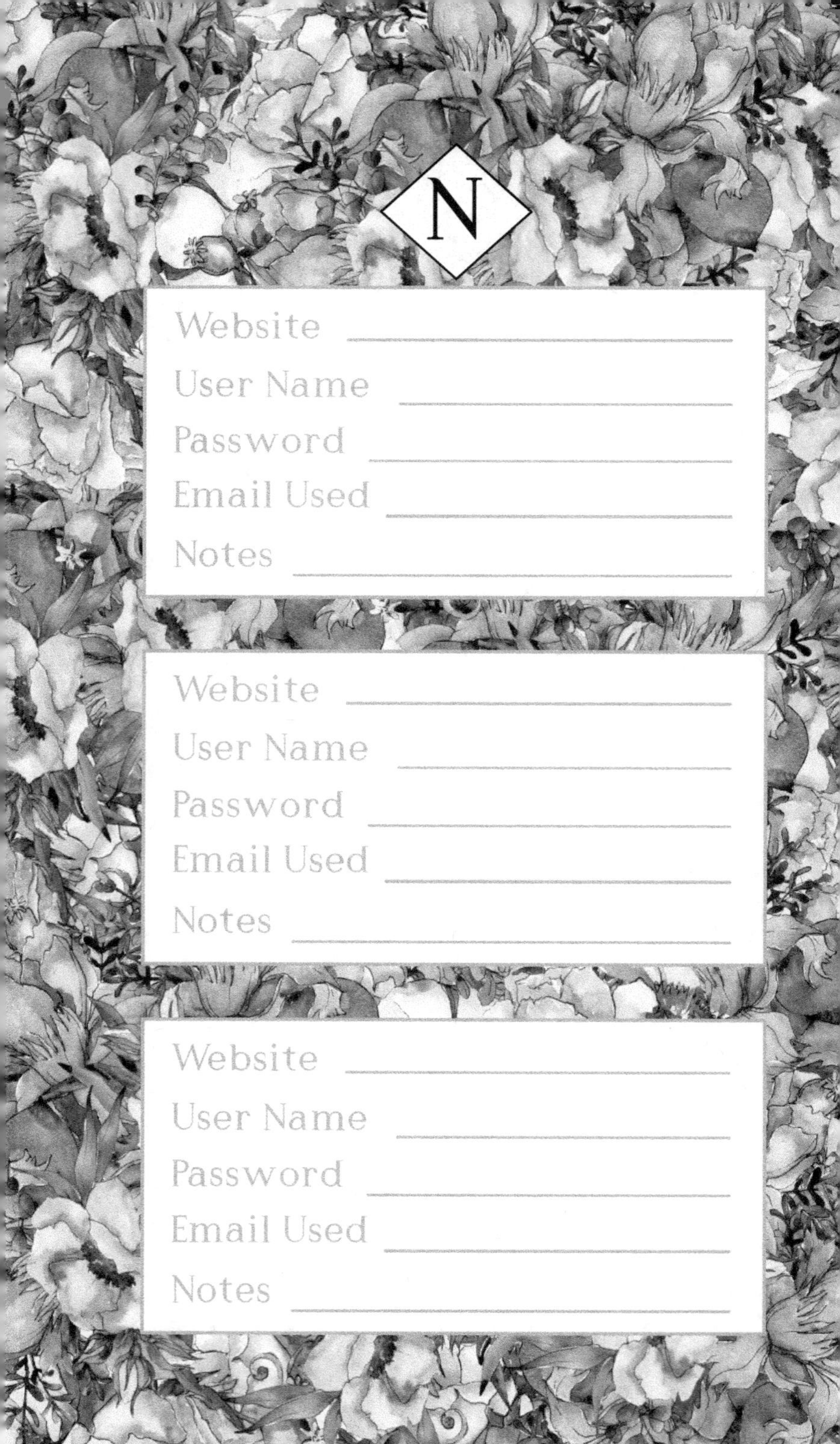

N

Website
User Name
Password
Email Used
Notes

Website
User Name
Password
Email Used
Notes

Website
User Name
Password
Email Used
Notes

N

Website
User Name
Password
Email Used
Notes

Website
User Name
Password
Email Used
Notes

Website
User Name
Password
Email Used
Notes

N

Website
User Name
Password
Email Used
Notes

Website
User Name
Password
Email Used
Notes

Website
User Name
Password
Email Used
Notes

O

Website
User Name
Password
Email Used
Notes

Website
User Name
Password
Email Used
Notes

Website
User Name
Password
Email Used
Notes

O

Website
User Name
Password
Email Used
Notes

Website
User Name
Password
Email Used
Notes

Website
User Name
Password
Email Used
Notes

O

Website

User Name

Password

Email Used

Notes

Website

User Name

Password

Email Used

Notes

Website

User Name

Password

Email Used

Notes

O

Website
User Name
Password
Email Used
Notes

Website
User Name
Password
Email Used
Notes

Website
User Name
Password
Email Used
Notes

P

Website
User Name
Password
Email Used
Notes

Website
User Name
Password
Email Used
Notes

Website
User Name
Password
Email Used
Notes

P

Website
User Name
Password
Email Used
Notes

Website
User Name
Password
Email Used
Notes

Website
User Name
Password
Email Used
Notes

P

Website
User Name
Password
Email Used
Notes

Website
User Name
Password
Email Used
Notes

Website
User Name
Password
Email Used
Notes

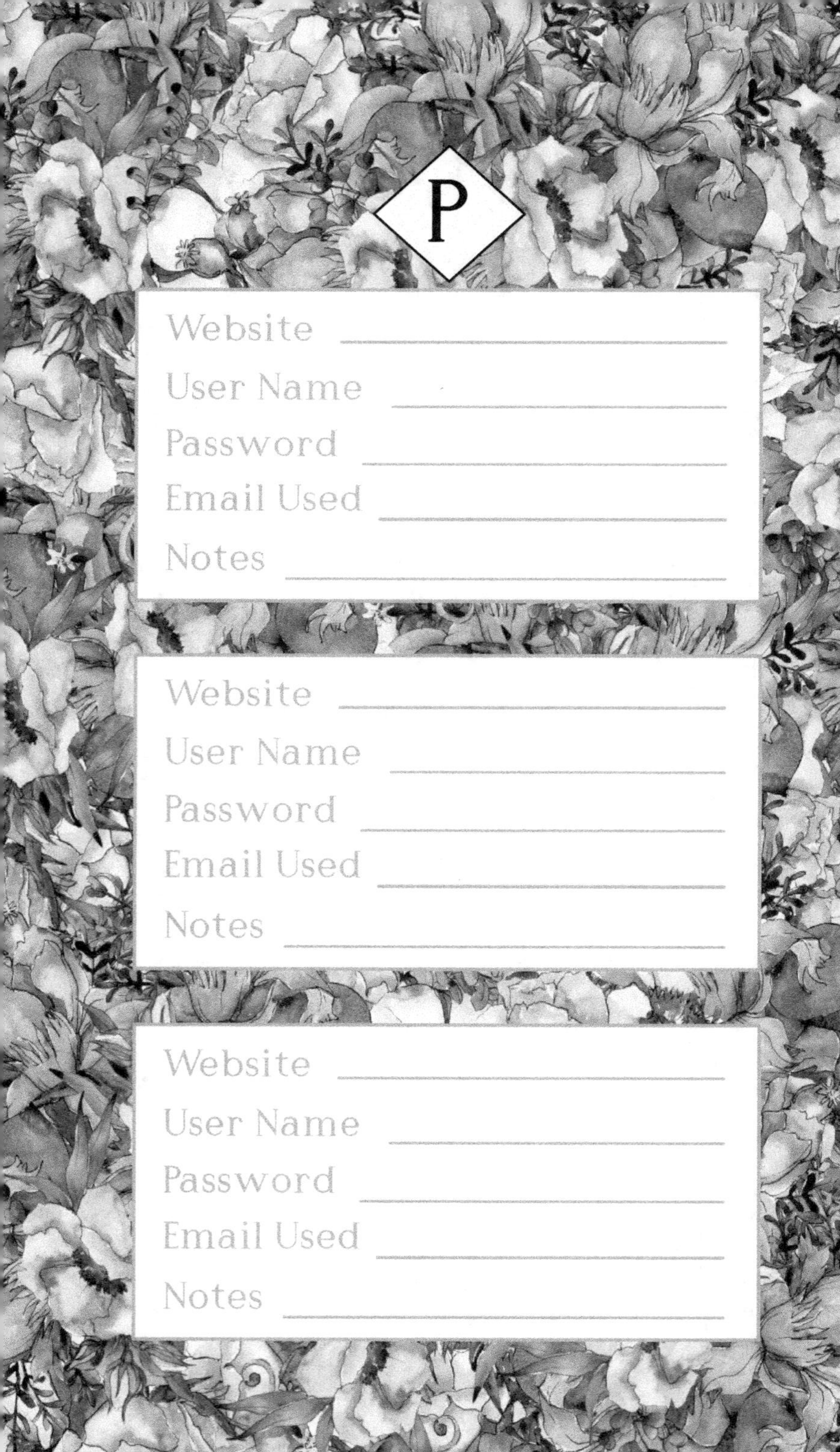

P

Website

User Name

Password

Email Used

Notes

Website

User Name

Password

Email Used

Notes

Website

User Name

Password

Email Used

Notes

Q

Website
User Name
Password
Email Used
Notes

Website
User Name
Password
Email Used
Notes

Website
User Name
Password
Email Used
Notes

Q

Website

User Name

Password

Email Used

Notes

Website

User Name

Password

Email Used

Notes

Website

User Name

Password

Email Used

Notes

Q

Website
User Name
Password
Email Used
Notes

Website
User Name
Password
Email Used
Notes

Website
User Name
Password
Email Used
Notes

Q

Website
User Name
Password
Email Used
Notes

Website
User Name
Password
Email Used
Notes

Website
User Name
Password
Email Used
Notes

R

Website
User Name
Password
Email Used
Notes

Website
User Name
Password
Email Used
Notes

Website
User Name
Password
Email Used
Notes

Website

User Name

Password

Email Used

Notes

Website

User Name

Password

Email Used

Notes

Website

User Name

Password

Email Used

Notes

R

Website
User Name
Password
Email Used
Notes

Website
User Name
Password
Email Used
Notes

Website
User Name
Password
Email Used
Notes

R

Website

User Name

Password

Email Used

Notes

Website

User Name

Password

Email Used

Notes

Website

User Name

Password

Email Used

Notes

# S

Website

User Name

Password

Email Used

Notes

Website

User Name

Password

Email Used

Notes

Website

User Name

Password

Email Used

Notes

S

Website
User Name
Password
Email Used
Notes

Website
User Name
Password
Email Used
Notes

Website
User Name
Password
Email Used
Notes

S

Website
User Name
Password
Email Used
Notes

Website
User Name
Password
Email Used
Notes

Website
User Name
Password
Email Used
Notes

S

Website
User Name
Password
Email Used
Notes

Website
User Name
Password
Email Used
Notes

Website
User Name
Password
Email Used
Notes

T

Website
User Name
Password
Email Used
Notes

Website
User Name
Password
Email Used
Notes

Website
User Name
Password
Email Used
Notes

T

Website

User Name

Password

Email Used

Notes

Website

User Name

Password

Email Used

Notes

Website

User Name

Password

Email Used

Notes

T

Website

User Name

Password

Email Used

Notes

Website

User Name

Password

Email Used

Notes

Website

User Name

Password

Email Used

Notes

T

Website

User Name

Password

Email Used

Notes

Website

User Name

Password

Email Used

Notes

Website

User Name

Password

Email Used

Notes

U

Website
User Name
Password
Email Used
Notes

Website
User Name
Password
Email Used
Notes

Website
User Name
Password
Email Used
Notes

U

Website
User Name
Password
Email Used
Notes

Website
User Name
Password
Email Used
Notes

Website
User Name
Password
Email Used
Notes

U

Website
User Name
Password
Email Used
Notes

Website
User Name
Password
Email Used
Notes

Website
User Name
Password
Email Used
Notes

U

Website

User Name

Password

Email Used

Notes

Website

User Name

Password

Email Used

Notes

Website

User Name

Password

Email Used

Notes

V

Website
User Name
Password
Email Used
Notes

Website
User Name
Password
Email Used
Notes

Website
User Name
Password
Email Used
Notes

V

Website
User Name
Password
Email Used
Notes

Website
User Name
Password
Email Used
Notes

Website
User Name
Password
Email Used
Notes

V

Website
User Name
Password
Email Used
Notes

Website
User Name
Password
Email Used
Notes

Website
User Name
Password
Email Used
Notes

V

Website

User Name

Password

Email Used

Notes

Website

User Name

Password

Email Used

Notes

Website

User Name

Password

Email Used

Notes

W

Website
User Name
Password
Email Used
Notes

Website
User Name
Password
Email Used
Notes

Website
User Name
Password
Email Used
Notes

W

Website
User Name
Password
Email Used
Notes

Website
User Name
Password
Email Used
Notes

Website
User Name
Password
Email Used
Notes

W

Website
User Name
Password
Email Used
Notes

Website
User Name
Password
Email Used
Notes

Website
User Name
Password
Email Used
Notes

W

Website
User Name
Password
Email Used
Notes

Website
User Name
Password
Email Used
Notes

Website
User Name
Password
Email Used
Notes

X

Website

User Name

Password

Email Used

Notes

Website

User Name

Password

Email Used

Notes

Website

User Name

Password

Email Used

Notes

X

Website
User Name
Password
Email Used
Notes

Website
User Name
Password
Email Used
Notes

Website
User Name
Password
Email Used
Notes

X

Website
User Name
Password
Email Used
Notes

Website
User Name
Password
Email Used
Notes

Website
User Name
Password
Email Used
Notes

# X

Website _______________

User Name _______________

Password _______________

Email Used _______________

Notes _______________

Website _______________

User Name _______________

Password _______________

Email Used _______________

Notes _______________

Website _______________

User Name _______________

Password _______________

Email Used _______________

Notes _______________

Y

Website

User Name

Password

Email Used

Notes

Website

User Name

Password

Email Used

Notes

Website

User Name

Password

Email Used

Notes

Y

Website
User Name
Password
Email Used
Notes

Website
User Name
Password
Email Used
Notes

Website
User Name
Password
Email Used
Notes

Y

Website
User Name
Password
Email Used
Notes

Website
User Name
Password
Email Used
Notes

Website
User Name
Password
Email Used
Notes

Y

Website
User Name
Password
Email Used
Notes

Website
User Name
Password
Email Used
Notes

Website
User Name
Password
Email Used
Notes

Z

Website

User Name

Password

Email Used

Notes

Website

User Name

Password

Email Used

Notes

Website

User Name

Password

Email Used

Notes

Z

Website
User Name
Password
Email Used
Notes

Website
User Name
Password
Email Used
Notes

Website
User Name
Password
Email Used
Notes

Z

Website

User Name

Password

Email Used

Notes

Website

User Name

Password

Email Used

Notes

Website

User Name

Password

Email Used

Notes

Z

Website
User Name
Password
Email Used
Notes

Website
User Name
Password
Email Used
Notes

Website
User Name
Password
Email Used
Notes